T0402875

EXPLODED BY SCIENCE

by Charis Mather

Minneapolis, Minnesota

Credits

All images are courtesy of Shutterstock.com, unless otherwise specified. With thanks to Getty Images, Thinkstock Photo, and iStockphoto. Front Cover – Teguh Mujiono, GraphicsRF.com, Arthur Balitskii. 4–5 – Veres Production, Gus And. 6–7 – PANG WRP, echoofthewaves, Slatan, Peter Gedeon, Robert P Horton, bc__astro, Roland Arhelger, CC BY-SA 4.0 <https://creativecommons.org/licenses/by-sa/4.0>, via Wikimedia Commons. 8–9 – Timothy Hodgkinson, Tatiana Bobkova, 24K-Production, User:Timpaananen, CC BY-SA 3.0 <https://creativecommons.org/licenses/by-sa/3.0>, via Wikimedia Commons. 10–11 – John A. Anderson, Flipser, Xiangli Li, Baiterek Media, Ivan Shmakov, CC0, via Wikimedia Commons. 12–13 – Dargaud, CC BY-SA 4.0 <https://creativecommons.org/licenses/by-sa/4.0>, via Wikimedia Commons, S_Photo, Lars-Goran Heden. 14–15 – Stockbym, jsp, Zde, CC BY-SA 4.0 <https://creativecommons.org/licenses/by-sa/4.0>, via Wikimedia Commons, Rebeca Ker Hoshen, steve estvanik. 16–17 – vangelis aragiannis, imagIN.gr photography, YuriiT, Council of Managers of National Antarctic Programs (COMNAP), CC BY-SA 3.0 <https://creativecommons.org/licenses/by-sa/3.0>, via Wikimedia Commons. 18–19 – Viacheslav Lopatin, RTimages, VIDEOMUNDUM. 20–21 – azure1, Dimitrios Karamitros, MID4552, Steve Mann, Merikanto, CC BY-SA 4.0 <https://creativecommons.org/licenses/by-sa/4.0>, via Wikimedia Commons. 22–23 – NickolayV, matrioshka, DanieleGay, Jarno Gonzalez Zarraonandia, Daniel Prudek. 24–25 – Stig Alenas, schankz, Vivvi Smak, Christian Vinces. 26–27 – Copula, Nikolay Zaborskikh, juan carlos tinjaca, schusterbauer.com. 28–29 – olpo, Alex DeCiccio, CC BY-SA 4.0 <https://creativecommons.org/licenses/by-sa/4.0>, via Wikimedia Commons, Nicolas-SB, Matt9122, Minerva Studio, Danny Ye, AROONA. 30 – feeling lucky.

Bearport Publishing Company Product Development Team

President: Jen Jenson; Director of Product Development: Spencer Brinker; Managing Editor: Allison Juda; Associate Editor: Naomi Reich; Associate Editor: Tiana Tran; Senior Designer: Colin O'Dea; Associate Designer: Elena Klinkner; Associate Designer: Kayla Eggert; Product Development Specialist: Anita Stasson

Library of Congress Cataloging-in-Publication Data is available at www.loc.gov or upon request from the publisher.

ISBN: 979-8-88822-003-0 (hardcover)
ISBN: 979-8-88822-187-7 (paperback)
ISBN: 979-8-88822-318-5 (ebook)

© 2024 BookLife Publishing
This edition is published by arrangement with BookLife Publishing.

For more information, write to Bearport Publishing, 5357 Penn Avenue South, Minneapolis, MN 55419.

CONTENTS

Welcome to TNT

TOTALLY NOT TRUE

There are many amazing things about our planet, but sometimes it's hard to tell if awe-inspiring Earth stories are true.

Evidence helps us find answers. But not all evidence can be believed. Let's use science to find out what we can trust, and then blow up anything that's totally not true.

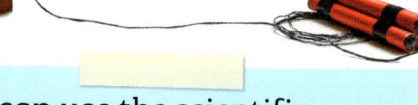

We can use the scientific method to **investigate** things we want to learn more about.

The Scientific Method

The scientific method uses these steps.

Step 1:
Ask a question.

Are there little worlds inside sea shells?

Step 2:
Make a guess.

Yes. I can hear sounds coming from inside a shell.

Step 3:
Find evidence.

I'll look for anything inside the shell.

Step 4:
Answer your question.

Nope. There wasn't anything in the shell.

Step 5:
Ask a new question, and do it again.

Why do I hear ocean waves when I put my hand over my ear?

Warning! Some evidence in this book may be misleading or have a different explanation. Look out for this stamp.

MISLEADING WARNING EVIDENCE

LET'S GET READY TO EXPLODE SOME MYTHS WITH SCIENCE!

Flat Earth

Some people don't believe scientists who say Earth is round. Instead, they think there's evidence that Earth is flat. Is it true?

Not curved!

LOOKS PRETTY STRAIGHT!

See the Seas

If Earth was round, wouldn't we be able to see the curve when we look far out into the distance? Whether peering at the open ocean or staring at giant walls of ice in the Antarctic, the distant edge of Earth looks flat.

Cloud Cover Up?

If the sun is really far away, why does it sometimes look like there are clouds behind it? Is the sun really much closer than people say? If so, it wouldn't light up very much of a round planet. However, it might give enough light to a flat world.

Clouds behind the sun!

Dome Sweet Dome?

Each night we can see the same **constellations** move across the sky. If Earth was round, wouldn't we see different groups of stars every night? Maybe the stars are stuck to the inside of a rotating **dome** that covers a flat Earth.

Chicago

On a round Earth it would be impossible to see things that are very far away. But the city of Chicago, Illinois, can be seen from the other side of Lake Michigan. If Earth is round, wouldn't Chicago be hidden behind the curve?

This group of three stars has moved!

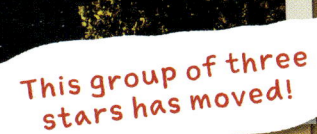

SCIENCE PROVES THAT FLAT EARTH IDEAS ARE WRONG. LET'S EXPLODE THEM!

Spotted from Space

Earth is very big. It's hard to see the large, curved surface from land. But astronauts can see it from space. Since 1960, those traveling to space have been able to look down at our round planet.

Through the Clouds

Thin clouds that pass in front of the sun are hard to see because the sun is so bright. It may look like the clouds are behind the sun, but this is just an **optical illusion**.

A bright enough light could easily shine through thin clouds, just like the light shining through this cloth.

8

We spin

Stars stay in place

We see stars in different places in the sky at different times because Earth is moving. The stars stay in place while Earth spins and moves through space. We see different stars depending on which way Earth is facing.

Optical Illusion

The light we see things with travels differently through air that is different temperatures. This bounces and bends images above water, making things behind Earth's curve visible. It makes Chicago look higher up from the planet's surface than it actually is.

The temperature difference can also make ships look like they are flying.

9

Climate Change

Scientists say Earth's climate is changing because of human actions. It is getting warmer. But some people don't believe this.

Record Cold

Global warming is supposed to be part of climate change. However, in 2021, Antarctica had a record cold winter with temperatures below -75 degrees Fahrenheit (-60 degrees Celsius). Some places have also been getting more snow each year.

Lots of snow in New York

Sea Ice Surge

Scientists have been watching sea ice for many years. They have found that there is more and more ice around Antarctica. If the climate is warming, why is there more ice?

Plenty of ice

MISLEADING WARNING EVIDENCE

Ups and Downs

We know world temperatures change naturally over time. In the past 1,000 years, the world was warmer during the Medieval Warm Period and colder during the Little Ice Age. These changes had nothing to do with people. The same thing could be happening now without any human cause.

During the Little Ice Age, the river Thames in London, England, would freeze over.

Power the Plants

Some say human-produced **carbon dioxide** is causing climate change. But plants need carbon dioxide to grow. More plants are good for the planet.

More carbon dioxide = more plants = cooler planet?

On the Rise

Climate change affects the whole world. It makes some places colder. But the overall temperature of Earth is warmer than it used to be.

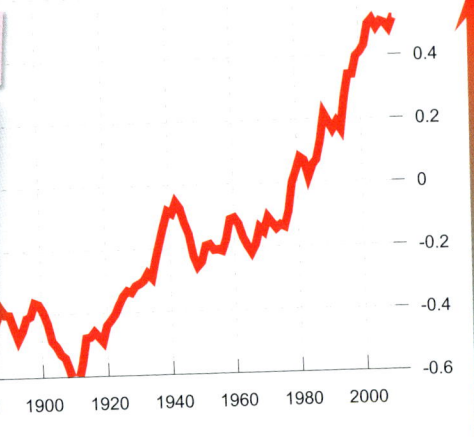

Hotter

0.6
0.4
0.2
0
-0.2
-0.4
-0.6

Colder

80 1900 1920 1940 1960 1980 2000

The Arctic, 1984

Russia

Greenland

I See the Sea Ice

The amount of sea ice in Antarctica has stayed about the same, but sea ice in the Arctic is melting more than it used to. We can see this in pictures taken from space.

Russia

The Arctic, 2012

Greenland

Canada

Not So Normal

While there have been natural temperature changes throughout history, they usually happen in smaller areas, not across the whole planet. Scientists can see this by looking at old ice and trees from different places.

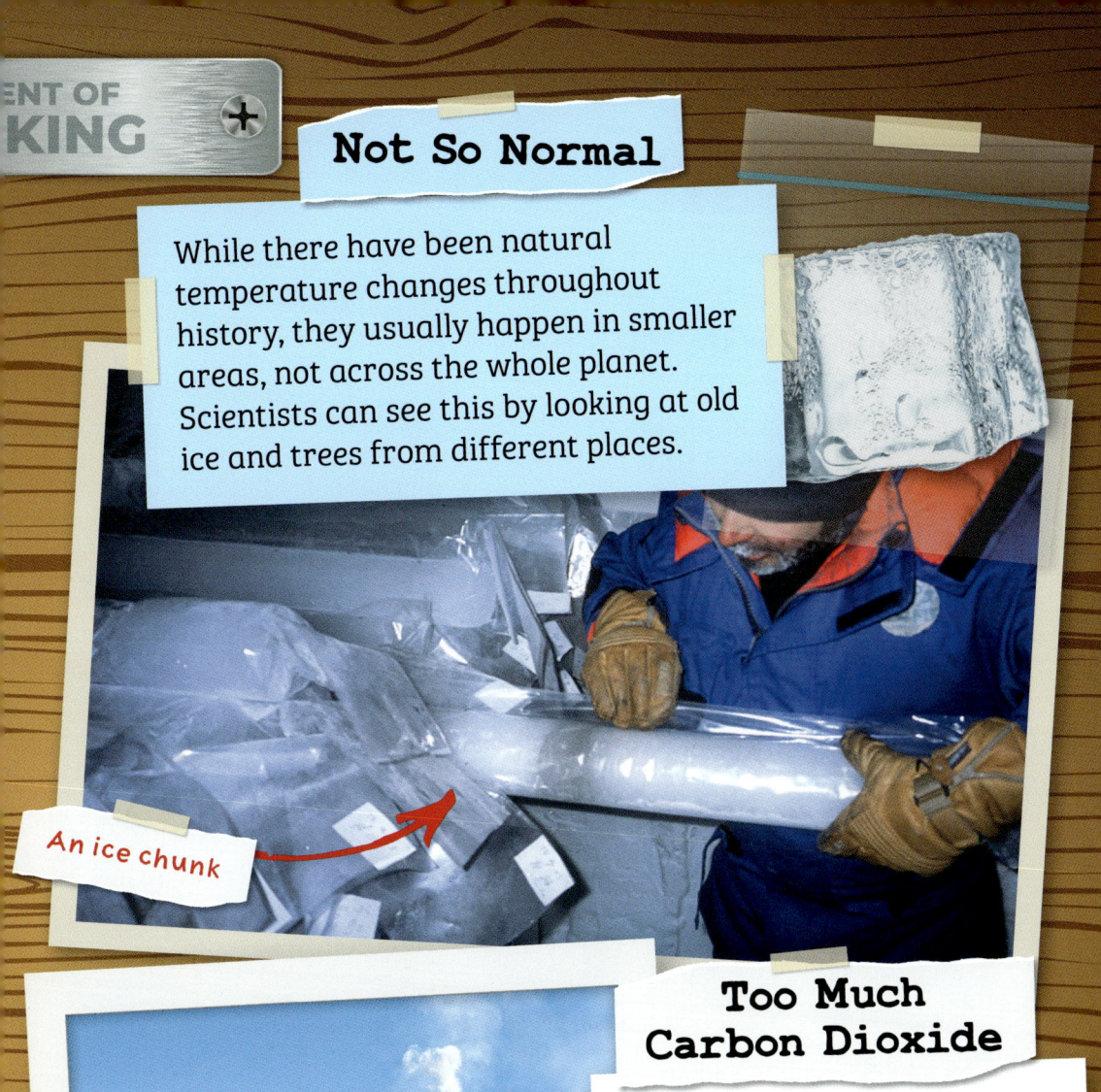

An ice chunk

Too Much Carbon Dioxide

Some carbon dioxide is good for plants, but humans are making more than plants can use. The extra carbon dioxide ends up in the sea and air. This can hurt the planet and the things living on it.

Too much carbon = bad for plants

13

Atlantis

There are stories of an ancient city called Atlantis. The city was lost thousands of years ago when it sank under the sea. Some people believe Atlantis was real and that its people had especially advanced **technology**.

Early written language

Ancient and Advanced?

How did early humans learn about advanced languages, metalworking, and farming? Could they have learned these things from the Atlanteans before they disappeared?

Ahead of Its Time

We may have found an example of Atlantean technology on a sunken ship! The Antikythera device is an ancient clock with complicated parts that shows an advanced knowledge of the stars.

Antikythera device

Santorini

In some stories about Atlantis, the city was built on islands that formed a ring with an island in the middle. Today, there is an island called Santorini that has a similar shape. People have found ancient **ruins** near it.

Are these ruins in Santorini actually Atlantean ruins?

Antarctica

If Atlantis isn't near Santorini, people think it might be in Antarctica! One ancient map shows that Antarctica may have been a warmer place a long time ago. Maybe Atlantis hasn't been found yet because it's covered by ice.

Did Atlanteans make a map of their home?

LET'S EXPLODE FALSE EVIDENCE OF ATLANTIS!

Just a Story

The story of Atlantis first came from just one person—Plato! He was known for using made-up stories to explain complicated ideas. **Experts** agree that his story wasn't true. And there aren't any historical records of Atlantis.

STORIES ARE MORE TRUSTWORTHY IF THEY COME FROM MORE THAN ONE PERSON.

The Greeks Might Disagree!

The Antikythera device was probably made by ancient Greeks. The ship it was found on had other Greek items, including the head from a statue of the Greek hero Hercules.

Greek pots from the ship

16

The Minoans

There was once an ancient group of people on Santorini, but they were **Minoans**, not Atlanteans. The Minoans were destroyed by huge waves caused by a volcano. The volcano also created the ring-shaped islands of the area.

Reading into It

Experts think the ancient map looks more like South America than Antarctica. There is also writing on the map that says it was made by people from Europe not Atlantis.

WHEN LOOKING FOR ANSWERS, DON'T IGNORE EVIDENCE!

Actually South America?

EXPLODED BY SCIENCE!

17

Bermuda Triangle

The Bermuda Triangle is a large area of ocean where many airplanes and ships have disappeared. Is the Bermuda Triangle cursed, or is there an otherworldly force at work here?

MISLEADING **WARNING** EVIDENCE

SOMETHING FISHY IS GOING ON!

Vincent Gaddis

In 1964, Vincent Gaddis made a list of many ships that had gone missing without explanation. He noticed many had disappeared in one area. He named it the Bermuda Triangle.

DAILY NEWS
World · Business · Finance · Lifestyle · Travel · Sport · Weather

BERMUDA: SHIPWRECK CAPITAL!

DAILY NEWS
World · Business · Finance · Lifestyle · Travel · Sport · Weather

BEWARE, ALL BERMUDA BOATERS. THE TRIANGLE HAS TAKEN ANOTHER VICTIM!

Shipwreck Capital

Bermuda has been called the shipwreck capital of the world because of its unusual number of sunken ships. More than 300 shipwrecks have been found there.

18

Flight 19

In 1945, a group of five U.S. airplanes, known as Flight 19, disappeared somewhere over the Bermuda Triangle. The planes, along with their 14 pilots, all disappeared at the same time.

The Flight 19 airplanes looked like this.

Even though he was an expert pilot, the group's leader hadn't been able to figure out where they were, even with a compass and other technology to help him. There was a huge search for Flight 19 after the planes went missing, but nothing was found.

What happened to Flight 19?

LET'S CLEAR THIS UP WITH A BANG.

Shocking Stories

Vincent Gaddis was a writer whose job was to make things sound more exciting and shocking than they were. He didn't look for evidence or check if the number of disappearances was actually unusual. Some ocean experts say the number is normal.

VINCENT GADDIS

The Gulf Stream

The shipwreck capital is in the path of quick-moving water that can pull things along with it. It's called the Gulf Stream. Sometimes, ships are dragged into **coral reefs** by the Gulf Stream.

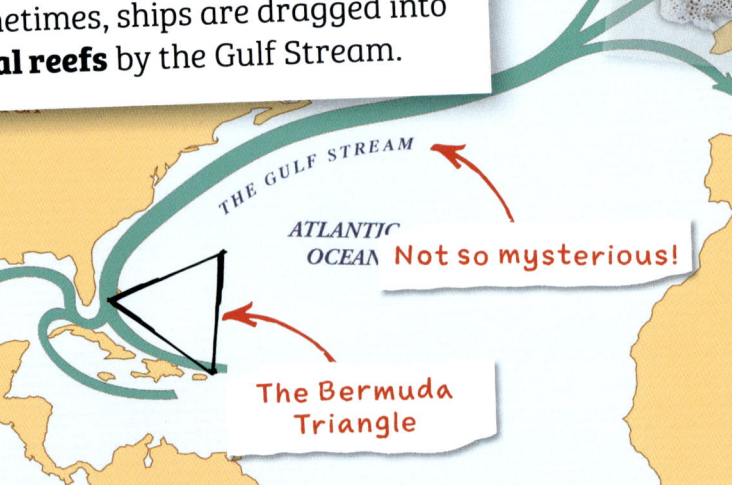

THE GULF STREAM

ATLANTIC OCEAN

Not so mysterious!

The Bermuda Triangle

EUROPE

AFRICA

SOUTH AMERICA

SCIENCE

Wrong?

Compass Trouble

Normally, compasses point north, but there are places in the world where compasses can be a little off. This happens in the Bermuda Triangle. Before he went missing, Flight 19's group leader reported that his compasses weren't working. This could be how he got lost.

Follow the Leader

Records from Flight 19 show that some of the other pilots believed the flight leader was going in the wrong direction. However, they had to follow their leader and may have done so until they all ran out of fuel.

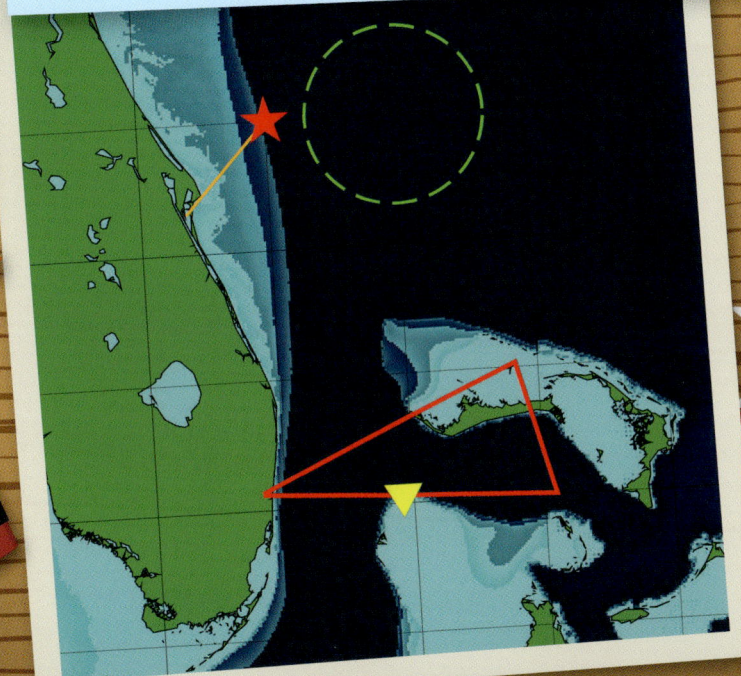

EXPLODED BY SCIENCE!

Ancient Aliens

There are some structures that are so amazing it seems impossible to think humans could have made them alone. Did they get help from aliens?

MISLEADING **WARNING** EVIDENCE

Pyramids

Although they are thousands of years old, the pyramids in Egypt are some of the most amazing structures on Earth. The largest pyramid was made from more than two million blocks. Experts still don't really know how they were built without modern technology.

Each block weighs more than a car!

Did aliens build the pyramids?

Stonehenge

Stonehenge is a mysterious circle of huge stones in England. Some stones came from 120 miles (200 km) away. How were these heavy stones moved before wheels existed? What could they be for?

Is it a UFO landing site?

Nazca Lines

Pilots flying over the Nazca desert in Peru noticed huge drawings made of differently colored soil and stones. They are so big the only way to see them fully is from above. However, these patterns were built thousands of years before humans made airplanes. Strange!

A monkey drawing

A spider drawing

GET READY TO EXPLODE SOME UNSCIENTIFIC IDEAS!

Pyramid Proof

Experts have proof that humans really did build the pyramids. The homes and graves of some of the people who worked on the pyramids have been found in villages nearby. Some of the grave stones include what the person's job was.

SCIENCE

An Egyptian worker village

The bones in the graves definitely came from humans, not aliens.

Definitely human teeth

Rolling Stones

Even without wheels, humans could have moved the Stonehenge stones by rolling them on logs. Alien technology wouldn't have been needed.

Possible!

Nazca Lines

Nazca pot

While we aren't completely sure why the Nazca drawings were made, we are sure they were made by people. Pieces of broken pots and a nearby village show that people lived close by. They may have made the drawings for **rituals**. It is possible these people viewed the art from high places or walked them as part of the rituals.

JUST BECAUSE WE DON'T UNDERSTAND SOMETHING, DOESN'T MEAN IT CAME FROM ALIENS!

EXPLODED BY SCIENCE!

Truth or TNT?

Are any of these strange things true?

Trees of Stone?

In some parts of the world, it is possible to find rocks that look like pieces of trees. Is it possible for wood to turn into stone?

Not wood!

Shark Volcano!

Volcanoes are mostly known for their **eruptions**. However, there is one volcano that's famous for being full of sharks!

Raining Fish?

There have long been reports of fish raining down from the sky. Some of these stories go back hundreds of years. Could this be true?

Raining fish in 1555

More fishy rain in 1876

Are Dinosaur Bones Fake?

Some people don't believe dinosaurs ever existed. How do we know the dinosaur bones and fossils in museums are real? Maybe they are tricks!

HOW MUCH IS TRUE? LET'S FIND OUT:

Trees Rock

Wood really can turn into stone! It's called petrified wood. This can happen when wood is soaked in water for millions of years. Often, it occurs when volcanoes bury wood in mud and ash.

FACT

You can still see the rings in the wood turned to stone!

Submarine Secrets

There really is a volcano full of sharks, but it might not be what you think. Kavachi is an underwater volcano. It is home to two different kinds of sharks.

A HAMMERHEAD SHARK

A SILKY SHARK

Spouting the Truth

It is possible for storms to rain fish. Sometimes, powerful **waterspouts** suck up water from the seas. A strong enough waterspout might suck up fish, too. Then, the storm could drop the fish over land.

A WATERSPOUT

Dinosaur replica

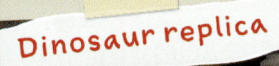

Reptile Replicas

While some dinosaur bones and fossils in museums are fake, dinosaurs themselves were very real. Museums show **replicas** so they can keep the real bones safe. There is lots of scientific evidence to prove dinosaurs really did exist.

Painting a replica

EXPLODED BY SCIENCE!

Scientific Solutions

It can be fun to believe in mysterious places that make ships and planes disappear, even if it isn't true. Sometimes, true stories, such as reports of raining fish, sound too silly to be real.

DAILY NEWS

World - Business - Finance - Lifestyle - Travel - Sport - Weather

BEWARE, ALL BERMUDA BOATERS. THE TRIANGLE HAS TAKEN ANOTHER VICTIM!

We can use the scientific method to figure out which stories are totally-not-true and need blowing up.

Next time you aren't sure what to believe, you'll know exactly what to do. . . . Blow up myths with science!

GLOSSARY

carbon dioxide a gas given off when fossil fuels are burned

constellations groups of stars that form a shape in the night sky

coral reefs rocklike structures formed from the skeletons of sea animals called coral polyps

dome a roof, shaped like half of a sphere

eruptions the explosion of volcanoes that usually throw out hot lava and ash with lots of force

evidence something that gives reason to believe another thing is true

experts people who know a lot about a subject

investigate to find evidence and learn a lot about something to try and find out the truth

Minoans ancient people who lived on an island off Greece

optical illusion something that tricks the eyes into seeing something a certain way

replicas models that look exactly like something

rituals special ceremonies for religious or other purposes

ruins what is left of something that has collapsed or been destroyed

technology the use of science to invent useful tools or to solve problems

waterspouts funnel clouds that rotate over water

INDEX

READ MORE

Harder, Megan. *Inside the Bermuda Triangle (Top Secret)*. Minneapolis: Lerner Publications, 2023.

Polinsky, Paige V. *Atlantis (Investigating the Unexplained)*. Minneapolis: Bellwether Media, 2020.

Thompson, V. C. *The Earth Is Flat (Conspiracy Theories: Debunked)*. Ann Arbor, MI: Cherry Lake Publishing, 2023.

LEARN MORE ONLINE

1. Go to **www.factsurfer.com** or scan the QR code below.
2. Enter "**Not True Earth**" into the search box.
3. Click on the cover of this book to see a list of websites.